rice

rice

clare ferguson

photography jeremy hopley

RYLAND
PETERS
& SMALL

LONDON NEW YORK

My thanks to Ian Ferguson,
my husband, for his forbearance.

Designer *Sarah Fraser*
Production *Paul Harding*
Art Director *Gabriella Le Grazie*
Publishing Director *Alison Starling*

Food Stylist *Clare Ferguson*
Prop Stylist *Wei Tang*

Notes
Rice is best served immediately after cooking.
If it is to be served cold, or reheated, it should be
cooled quickly after cooking, covered, chilled as fast
as possible in the coldest part of the refrigerator, and
used within 24 hours.

The herbs in this book are measured in bunches.
A large bunch consists of about 15 stems,
and a small bunch about 5 stems.

Rice has a subtle taste and requires assertive
seasoning with salt, soy sauce, fish sauce, or other
salty-tasting agents.

First published in the USA in 2004
by Ryland Peters & Small, Inc.
519 Broadway, 5th Floor
New York, NY 10012
www.rylandpeters.com

10 9 8 7 6 5 4 3 2 1

Text © Clare Ferguson 1997, 2004

Design and photographs © Ryland Peters & Small 1997, 2004

Printed and bound in China

Library of Congress Cataloging-in-Publication Data

Ferguson, Clare.
  Rice / Clare Ferguson ; photography by Jeremy Hopley.
    p. cm.
  ISBN 1-84172-717-2
  1. Cookery (Rice) I. Title.
  TX809.R5F45 2004
  641.6'318--dc22

                                        2003025076

Recipes in this book have previously been published in
Rice: from Risotto to Sushi by Clare Ferguson.

contents

how to cook rice

The best methods for cooking rice range from the most traditional to the most up-to-date and high-tech!

Measuring Rice and Water

The easiest method is by volume: take one container of rice and then add multiples of that container of hot water or stock; 1½ times for sushi rice, 2 for most other kinds of rice, 3 for risotto, or 4 for paella. Bring to a boil, cover the pan, reduce the heat, simmer until done— usually, though not always, for 12 minutes. This method, translated into ounces and cups, is used in this book. Alternatively, for boiled rice, cover the rice with liquid to a depth of one finger joint above the rice. Boil, cover, reduce heat, then simmer until done.

Absorption Method

Cover rice with boiling liquid. Return to a boil, uncovered. Cover, reduce immediately to the lowest possible heat. Avoid lifting the lid. After 10, 12, 15, or 25 minutes, or as listed in the recipes (depending on rice type), it will be cooked and all liquid absorbed. Steam holes may appear on the surface. Turn heat off. Serve immediately, or let stand, covered, for a few minutes to let the grains fluff up and lighten.

Pan-of-Water Method

Measure rice into a large saucepan. Add copious boiling water or stock. Do not cover. Return to a boil, reduce to a medium simmer, and cook 10, 12, 15, 25, or more minutes, appropriate to the rice type, or until tender. Turn off the heat and strain. Return to the pan, let stand for a few minutes, then serve.

Electric Rice Cookers

These convenient, foolproof machines make cooking rice child's play. You should follow the instructions given with each machine, but the usual method is to measure the rice, then add the level of water relevant to that type. Add no salt. Cover and switch on. When the rice is done, the machine turns off automatically and the rice will keep hot for up to 1 hour.

Cooking Rice in a Microwave

Though no faster than conventional methods, it is useful, since the machine automatically turns off and residual heat warms and fluffs up the rice. Choose a large, medium height, non-metal microwaveable casserole or covered bowl. Add 1 scoop (e.g. 1 cup) rice. Measure in 1¾ scoops of liquid for sushi rice, 2 for white or brown rice, 3 for Camargue and Thai red rice, wild rice, or risotto rice, and 4 for calasparra or bomba rice. Cover. For all kinds of rice, in 750 watt models, microwave on HIGH/FULL for 10 minutes or until boiling. Then, for white rice, reduce to MEDIUM/50% for 5 minutes. For wild, brown, and Camargue red rice, reduce to MEDIUM/50%, cook 30 minutes, let stand 5 minutes. For Thai red rice, reduce to MEDIUM/50%, cook 20 minutes, let stand for 5 minutes. Easy-cook rice of any variety will take 3–4 minutes longer at MEDIUM/50% than the untreated form of that variety. To reheat previously cooked rice, cover and microwave on HIGH/FULL for 3–4 minutes (or 6–8 minutes for wild or brown rice).

Note: These timings are for a 750 watt model. If yours is of higher wattage, deduct 10 seconds per minute of the recipe for every 100 watts. If lower, add 10 seconds per minute of the recipe for each 100 watts.

Cooking in a Pressure Cooker

Useful for brown rice. Specific instructions should be followed for each model, but this is the general method. Leave the low trivet in position. Add the measured rice. Cover with boiling water or stock. Set the lid in position, bring to a gentle simmer, turn the pressure gauge to the higher pressure, reduce the heat, and leave to cook. Turn off and remove the pan from the heat. Allow the steam vent to reduce its plume of steam, then let the pan and its contents cool enough for the pressure to reduce. Uncover.

Cooking Rice in the Oven

A good but rather slow method, used for English rice pudding, where rice, sugar, eggs, and milk are cooked in a moderate oven for 50 minutes.

Steamed Rice

When Asian cooks or restaurants specify "steamed rice," they may well mean rice cooked in boiling water and steam by the absorption method or even in an electric rice cooker. Traditional Southeast Asian recipes for steamed sticky rice may need specific methods relevant to those cultures, where rice cooking is taken to a high art. Follow the recipe instructions, or adapt the method to the utensils you have available.

snacks and appetizers

One of the glories of the Japanese kitchen, sushi traditionally involves much ritual, but it is possible to apply the general principles using Western utensils. The essentials are Japanese short grain sushi rice and other authentic ingredients. Most supermarkets and natural food stores stock sushi rice, *kombu* (dried kelp), *nori* (sheets of dried seaweed), rice vinegar, black sesame seeds, *umeboshi* (pickled plums), *wasabi* paste (green horseradish), and pink pickled ginger. Shown here and overleaf are three sushi made with two methods, using rolls or balls of rice.

sumeshi

2 cups sushi rice, washed and drained

8-inch piece *kombu* (dried kelp)

⅓ cup Japanese rice vinegar

2 tablespoons sugar

2 teaspoons sea salt

3 inches fresh ginger, finely sliced

3 garlic cloves, crushed

to serve

¼ cup Japanese soy sauce

2 oz. Japanese *wasabi* paste

4 oz. pickled pink ginger

onigiri

1 portion *sumeshi* (vinegared rice)

4 oz. lightly cooked salmon fillet

6 *umeboshi* (pickled plums)

1 sheet *nori* (dried seaweed)

serves 6

japanese sushi

Sumeshi, or vinegared rice, is the basis of all Japanese sushi. This recipe gives enough rice to make 3 different kinds of sushi; *onigiri* (stuffed balls of rice patted into squares, with seaweed squares top and bottom), *norimaki* (sushi rolls), and *gungamaki* (a plain, rice-filled sushi roll, tapped until rectangular in section, then cut into slices and topped with fresh seafood).

Sumeshi

To prepare the rice, put it in a saucepan with the *kombu* and 2¾ cups boiling water. Simmer, covered, for 18 minutes until steam holes appear in the surface. Let stand 5 minutes. Mix the vinegar, sugar, salt, ginger, and garlic, and stir into the rice. Divide into 3 portions. Use one portion to make each of the 3 kinds of sushi shown here.

Onigiri

Using wet hands, pinch, squeeze, and pat one portion of the rice into 6 even balls. Push a hole in each ball. Put some salmon and a plum inside. Close the rice and squeeze back into shape. Continue to make 5 more. Cut the nori sheet into 12 squares. Set one piece on top of each rice ball and one under. Pat gently to make 6 squares. Serve.

1 egg, beaten

1 pinch of powdered saffron
(optional)

1 teaspoon peanut oil

4 sheets *nori* (dried seaweed),
lightly toasted over a gas flame

1 portion *sumeshi* (vinegared rice)

2 inches cucumber,
cut into 8 thin wedges

½ red bell pepper, sliced lengthwise

4 scallions, halved lengthwise

serves 6

Norimaki

To make the omelette, put the egg, 1 tablespoon water, and saffron in a bowl and beat with a fork. Heat a skillet, add the oil, then pour in the egg mixture. Cook both sides until set but not browned. Cool, then cut in half. Put 2 sheets of toasted *nori* on 2 sheets of plastic wrap (instead of the traditional bamboo mat). Add half the portion of rice to each and spread in an even layer on top of the *nori*, leaving a narrow margin at the far edge.

Add the omelet, cucumber, pepper, and scallions, as shown. Roll up the *nori*, pulling away the plastic as you go. As each roll is complete, wrap it in plastic, and secure the ends with elastic bands. Cut into 1-inch slices. Remove and discard the plastic. Serve.

1 portion *sumeshi* (vinegared rice)

2 sheets *nori* (dried seaweed) lightly toasted over a gas flame

4 uncooked shrimp tails, blanched

4 pieces sushi-grade salmon, ¼ oz. each

2 oz. keta or saviar (salmon roe)

1 teaspoon black sesame seeds

6 chives

serves 6

Gungamaki (Battleship Rolls)

Make 2 plain sushi rolls—with no filling—using the rice and *nori*, following the method on the previous page. Tap the sides of the rolls to form rectangles. Cut each roll into 6.

Remove the shrimp legs, if any, and snip up the belly with kitchen shears. Open out, snip off the shell above the tail, then press flat as shown.

Top the rectangles with salmon, salmon roe, and shrimp. Snip the salmon and shrimp to neaten the edges. Add sesame seeds and chives to the salmon. Serve all the sushi with the soy sauce, wasabi, and pink pickled ginger.

stuffed vegetables
with rice and sour cherries

4 large beefsteak tomatoes, with the tops sliced off and reserved

4 large red bell peppers with stems

2 tablespoons butter ghee

2 garlic cloves, chopped

2 onions, chopped

8 oz. twice-ground lamb

2 cinnamon sticks, crushed

1 teaspoon ground turmeric

1 teaspoon cumin seeds, crushed

1 teaspoon cracked black pepper

1 teaspoon sumak (optional)

2 oz. dried cranberries

½ cup basmati, or other long-grain rice

½ cup bulghur wheat

3 cups chicken stock

½ teaspoon salt

to serve

8 oz. plain yogurt

2 teaspoons dried mint
or 2 tablespoons sliced fresh mint

8 sprigs of mint

pita or other flatbreads

serves 4

Persian seasonings are fascinating and refreshing. This dish has a spicing mixture which hinges on pepper, cinnamon and mint, with turmeric, cumin, and sumak, a red-brown souring powder. All ingredients are available in Middle Eastern food stores and larger supermarkets.

Scoop the tomato pulp and seeds into a blender. Put the tomato shells and peppers in a roasting pan and cook in a preheated oven at 400°F for 10 minutes.

Meanwhile, heat the butter ghee in a heavy skillet and sauté the garlic, onions, lamb, cinnamon, turmeric, cumin, black pepper, and sumak, if using, for 5–6 minutes over high heat, stirring regularly. Blend the tomato pulp and seeds in the blender, then add to the pan together with the dried cranberries, rice, bulghur wheat, and 2¾ cups of the stock. Season with the salt. Return to a boil, cover, then simmer for 10 minutes.

Spoon the mixture into the vegetable shells and spoon 1 tablespoon of reserved stock over each. Set the sliced tops back on top of the tomatoes. Cover the dish with a double layer of foil and return to the oven. Reduce the oven heat to 350°F and cook for 40–45 minutes or until the rice is plumped up, all liquid is absorbed and the vegetables smell sweetly aromatic.

Serve hot with a spoonful of yogurt on top. Sprinkle with fresh or dried mint and serve with sprigs of mint and flatbreads to mop up the juices.

greek dolmathes

This vegetarian version of the classic dish came from the Greek island of Zante, where dried fruits are a major crop. Serve dolmathes as part of a mixed *meze* with feta, olives, and pickled chiles and always with a bowl of plain yogurt.

8 oz. fresh vine leaves, or preserved vine leaves, drained (about 50–60)

3 medium onions, quartered and finely sliced

5–6 scallions or baby leeks, trimmed and finely sliced

a large bunch of fresh herbs, such as parsley, mint, and/or dill, chopped

⅔ cup extra virgin olive oil

¾ cup long-grain white rice, soaked briefly in cold water

⅓ cup currants

½ cup pine nuts

freshly squeezed juice of 1 lemon

2½–3 cups boiling vegetable stock

2 teaspoons salt

sea salt and freshly ground black pepper

to serve

1 tub Greek yogurt, about 1 cup

2 lemons, cut into wedges

makes about 45–55, serves 6–8

If using brine-preserved leaves, put them in a colander set in a bowl under cold running water until the bowl is half full. Agitate them, then let drain. If using fresh leaves, blanch 5–6 at a time for about 1 minute in a large saucepan of boiling salted water. Rinse in cold water and drain in a colander.

Mix the onions and scallions with the herbs, half the oil, and the drained rice. Season with salt and pepper to taste. Stir in the currants, pine nuts, and the lemon juice. Put 1 heaping teaspoon of filling at the stalk end of one leaf. Roll up this end, then fold the side flaps over towards the center, neatly but not too tightly. Roll up, keeping the seam underneath, leaving room for expansion. Repeat until all the filling has been used.

Put half the remaining leaves in a large saucepan, flameproof casserole, or skillet, overlapping each leaf. Pack in the dolmathes in concentric circles. Cover with the remaining leaves and a flat, heatproof plate. Pour in boiling stock until just covered, add the 2 teaspoons salt, then bring to the boil, cover, reduce the heat, and simmer for 45–55 minutes or until the rice is sticky, swollen, and tender. Let stand undisturbed for 10 minutes. Drain if necessary.

Serve hot or warm, but not chilled. Sprinkle with the remaining oil and serve with yogurt and lemon wedges.

supplì cheese balls
with basil and pine nuts

Supplì are rice balls, cooked to pleasing crispness outside, melting inside. The melted mozzarella cheese oozes strings, the origin of their charming Italian name, *supplì al telefono*, or telephone "wires." Use leftover risotto or other cooked round-grain rice. The key thing is to ensure that the rice, at the outset, is well flavored: under-seasoned *supplì* are disappointing.

½ cup pine nuts

4 cups seasoned, cooked risotto rice

2 large eggs, beaten

a bunch of basil, finely sliced

3 oz. prosciutto, thinly sliced, cut into 36 squares

4 oz. mozzarella cheese, cut into 36 little strips

1 cup dry bread crumbs

olive oil, for frying

makes about 36, serves 6–8

Preheat the broiler, line the broiler pan with foil, and toast the pine nuts, shaking them occasionally under the heat until they are evenly golden brown.

Put the rice in a bowl, then fold in the pine nuts, eggs, and basil. Mix well. Using clean hands, shape into about 36 walnut-size balls. Use your index finger to push a hole in the center of each one. Insert a piece of prosciutto, followed by a piece of mozzarella. Pinch closed and squeeze the ball back into shape. Roll each ball in bread crumbs, then chill.

Heat the oil in a deep-fryer or saucepan to 375°F or until a cube of bread turns golden brown in 40 seconds. Using a frying basket, cook several balls at a time, rolling them around and turning them over with tongs, so that they are evenly golden brown all over (about 3 minutes). Make sure there is enough oil to cover them, or they may split during cooking because of uneven expansion.

Drain on crumpled paper towels and keep hot until all the balls are cooked. Serve hot as an appetizer, or as party food.

A glorious, sunshine-colored Provençal soup, using the dry, brilliantly orange-fleshed pumpkin (*calabaza*, in Caribbean markets), with its dark, heavy rind, firm flesh, and hard seeds. You could substitute a firm, dense squash, such as Hubbard or butternut, but not watery summer squash. Rice, garlic, and chiles add body, but the natural sweetness means good seasoning is very important, to balance the flavors.

pumpkin chowder
with rice and thyme

2½ lb. orange-fleshed pumpkin, peeled and seeded (about 2 lb.)

1 large Spanish onion, sliced

2½ cups well-seasoned chicken stock

1 teaspoon dried crushed chiles

1½ teaspoons salt

1 cinnamon stick, broken

a small bunch of thyme, plus extra to serve

1 fresh bay leaf, bruised

½ cup white long-grain rice

1¼ cups whole milk

sea salt and freshly ground black pepper

serves 6

Cut the pumpkin into cubes and put in a saucepan. Add the onion, stock, chiles, salt, cinnamon, thyme, and bay leaf. Bring to a boil, cover with a lid, and cook for 20 minutes or until done.

Meanwhile, put the rice in another saucepan and add boiling water to cover by 1 inch. Bring to a boil, cover with a lid, reduce the heat, and simmer for 15 minutes until most of the water has been absorbed.

When the vegetables are soft and pulpy, remove and discard the bay leaf and thyme. Reserve the cinnamon.

Using a blender, purée the soup in batches to a creamy consistency. (A food processor will give a less silky texture.) Return to the rinsed pan.

Add the drained rice and milk, then add salt and pepper to taste. Bring to a boil, simmer for 5 minutes, and serve with extra thyme sprinkled over the top, and a few reserved shards of the cinnamon.

Note This chowder may be served chilled, with hot garlic or herb bread, or fougasse, the lacy Provençal bread.

lobster and lemon risotto

A superbly luxurious taste of the sea. If you have time,
make stock from the lobster shells, but you can also use
either fresh fish stock or fish stock cubes.

1 cooked lobster, about 1½ lb.

2 tablespoons extra virgin olive oil

4 tablespoons salted butter

2 leeks, white parts only, finely sliced

2 cups white Italian risotto rice, such as carnaroli, arborio, or vialone nano

⅔ cup dry white wine

5 cups hot fish stock

1 unwaxed lemon

to serve

8 oz. mixed bitter greens, such as watercress and rocket

½ teaspoon mild paprika

serves 4

To prepare the lobster, crack open the claws and extract the meat. Cut open the body and tail and remove the edible meat in pieces as large as possible. Discard the inedible parts. Cut the tail meat into thick slices.

To make the risotto, heat the oil and half the butter in a medium saucepan. Add the leeks and sauté gently for 1–2 minutes. Add the rice, stir until well coated, then add the wine. Let it bubble.

Add a quarter of the hot stock and stir gently. Cook over gentle heat for 6–7 minutes, stirring now and then, until the liquid has been absorbed. Continue to add ladles of stock 3–4 times more until it has all been used. The risotto should be tender, but rich, moist, and glossy.

Cut the zest from the lemon into 4 long strips, curl the strips into twists, and set aside. Squeeze the juice from the lemon. Add the remaining butter to the risotto, followed by lemon juice to taste. Stir, cover with a lid, and heat through.

To serve, put a tangle of salad leaves on each plate and spoon the risotto on top. Put the lobster meat on top of the risotto, sprinkle with paprika, add a twist of lemon zest, and serve hot.

Italian risotto is remarkably straightforward as long as you use top-quality ingredients. Fresh butter, best risotto rice such as carnaroli or arborio, a glass of good wine, and well-flavored stock are essentials.

risotto alla milanese
saffron risotto

6 tablespoons salted butter

1 medium onion, sliced

3–4 garlic cloves, crushed (optional)

2 cups white Italian risotto rice

½ cup white wine

1 large pinch of saffron threads

¼ teaspoon sea salt (or, if stock is salty, sugar)

1 quart boiling chicken stock

3 oz. fresh Parmesan cheese, finely sliced

freshly ground black pepper

sprigs of flat-leaf parsley, to serve

serves 4

Heat 4 tablespoons of the butter in a medium saucepan. Add the onion and garlic, if using, sauté gently for 1 minute, then stir in the rice and wine. Let it bubble away.

Put the saffron and salt or sugar in a small bowl and grind with the back of a spoon. Add a ladle of stock. Pour half this mixture into the rice and reserve the remainder. Continue simmering the rice, adding ladles of boiling stock at intervals, until all the liquid has been used and absorbed (about 28 minutes). The risotto should be tender but still very rich, moist, and glossy. Alternatively, add all the stock at once and cook over low heat for 28–32 minutes, stirring gently from time to time.

Add the remaining butter and saffron, then stir in half the cheese and some pepper. To serve, sprinkle with the remaining cheese and the parsley.

rice pie with fruit salsa

5 oz. ready-made pastry dough, thawed if frozen, then chilled

1 heaping cup white easy-cook long-grain rice

¼ cup sweet chile sauce

1 tablespoon wasabi paste

⅔ cup sweet dessert wine

2 inches fresh ginger, finely sliced

1 teaspoon black onion seeds (nigella) (optional)

fruit salsa

4 ripe feijoas or kiwifruit

2 scallions, finely sliced

1 red serrano chile, sliced

2 garlic cloves, crushed

a large bunch of fresh flat-leaf parsley, cut with kitchen shears

2 tablespoons Asian fish sauce

2 teaspoons vanilla sugar

2 tablespoons rice vinegar

salt and freshly ground black pepper

salad leaves, to serve

a deep 8-inch tart pan, fluted or plain

parchment paper and baking beans or pie weights

serves 6–8

Rice in a pie? The idea may seem odd, but this brasserie-style dish is fascinating. A fresh salsa is the second surprise—feijoas are green tropical fruit with a superb, scented taste. As an alternative, kiwifruit taste different, but have similar texture.

Put the dough on a work surface and roll it out very thinly. Use to line the tart pan (don't worry about untidy edges—they become crisp and can be broken off later). Prick the base with a fork. Line the pie crust with parchment paper and baking beans or pie weights. Bake towards the top of a preheated oven at 400°F for 15 minutes. Remove the paper and beans and cook for a further 10 minutes or until the crust is golden and crisp.

As soon as the crust goes into the oven, cook the rice with about twice its volume (2 cups) of boiling water for 15–18 minutes, until the water is absorbed, steam holes appear in the top, and the rice is fluffy. Let stand for 5 minutes, covered.

Put the chile sauce, *wasabi* paste, and wine in a bowl and stir to dissolve. Add the ginger. Stir the mixture lightly through the rice. Remove the cooked pie crust from the oven and spoon in the seasoned rice—level the surface, but don't pack it heavily. Sprinkle the black onion seeds, if using, over the top. Set aside.

To make the salsa, cut the feijoas in half crosswise and scoop out the flesh with a teaspoon into a small bowl. Discard the skins. (If using kiwifruit, prepare in the same way.) Add the scallions, chile, garlic, parsley, fish sauce, sugar, and vinegar. Add salt and pepper to taste.

Serve warm or cool, but not chilled, cut in wedges with a spoonful of salsa on top and a few salad leaves. It should be served the day of making.

entrées

rice sticks
with szechuan-style sauce

⅔ cup peanut oil

½ cup shelled raw peanuts

2 teaspoons Szechuan peppercorns

1 small onion, chopped

2 garlic cloves, crushed

1¼ cups freshly made, strong, hot China tea, or green tea

2 tablespoons dark soy sauce

1–2 tablespoons dark sesame oil

2 inches fresh ginger, peeled and finely sliced

2 teaspoons mild paprika

3–4 dried bird's eye chiles, crumbled

freshly squeezed juice of 1 lemon

rice stick salad

2 cooked chicken breasts

1 cup snow peas

6–8 green lettuce leaves

1½ cups finely sliced carrots

1 cup finely sliced celery, with some leaves reserved

8 oz. dried rice stick noodles

a bunch of cilantro, torn

serves 4

Rice sticks, made from rice flour, are dried noodles packed in large skeins. The noodles are about ¼ inch wide, and are a great pantry standby item—very versatile and easy to prepare. Szechuan peppercorns—scented and spicy, rather than hot—are available from Chinese food stores or specialist spice merchants.

Heat the oil in a wok to about 375°F, or until a cube of bread browns in 40 seconds. Add the peanuts and Szechuan peppercorns and cook, stirring, for 1½ minutes. Empty the pan into a metal strainer set over a heatproof bowl. (This prevents the nuts overcooking and scorching.) Put the contents of the strainer, plus 2 tablespoons of the cooking oil, into a food processor with the onion, garlic, and half the hot tea. Blend to a paste. Add the remaining tea, soy sauce, sesame oil, ginger, paprika, chiles, and lemon juice, and blend again to make a sauce.

Pull the cooked chicken into shreds, or cut into cubes, and finely slice the snow peas and lettuce. Put the chicken, snow peas, lettuce, carrots, and celery in a pan with some salted boiling water. Cook for 2 minutes, drain, and discard the liquid.

Meanwhile, pour boiling water over the noodles and let soak for 3–4 minutes or until white and firm. Drain.

Just before serving, reheat by pouring over boiling water, then drain quickly. Put the rice stick noodles in a bowl, add the vegetables, chicken, and sauce, and toss well. Sprinkle with the torn cilantro and reserved celery leaves and serve.

malay noodle soup

8 oz. dried rice stick noodles

12 oz. uncooked shrimp tails

2 cups bean sprouts

1 tablespoon light soy sauce

1¾ cups canned coconut milk

8 oz. ready-made fish balls

1 small cucumber

a large bunch of fresh mint

4 lettuce leaves

rempah seasoning

2 inches fresh ginger, peeled

8 cashews, or macadamias

1–2 dried red chiles

1 stalk of lemongrass,
outer 2 leaves removed

1 tablespoon coriander seeds

¼ cup peanut oil

2 garlic cloves, slivered

8 shallots or 2 onions, sliced

2 teaspoons hot paprika

2 tablespoons Asian fish sauce

2 teaspoons ground turmeric

4 oz. dried shrimp

serves 4–6

Go to a Southeast Asian or Chinese supermarket for the various authentic ingredients. Don't be put off by the list—going shopping is half the fun!

To make the rempah seasoning, slice the ginger, chop the cashews, seed and chop the chiles, finely slice the lemongrass, and crush the coriander seeds. Heat the peanut oil in a small wok or saucepan, add all the rempah ingredients and stir-fry for 5 minutes.

To make the soup, put the rice stick noodles in a bowl, cover with boiling water, let soak for 5 minutes, then drain carefully and ladle the noodles into 4–6 small bowls or 1 large bowl.

Put the shrimp in a large saucepan with the bean sprouts, soy sauce, coconut milk, and fish balls. Add 1½ quarts boiling water and simmer for 5 minutes.

Cut the cucumber into 2-inch strips, finely slice the lettuce, and tear the mint leaves. Set aside.

Add a ladle of the boiling soup to the rempah mixture in the wok, then stir this mixture back into the soup and simmer for 6–7 minutes. Put the cucumber, lettuce, and mint on top of the noodles.

Reheat the pan of soup to near boiling, stirring to prevent the coconut milk from separating. Ladle the hot broth into the bowls—this will instantly reheat the noodles. Serve hot while all the colors, tastes, and textures are still vivid.

orange and pumpkin pulao

with two kashumbers and a raita

4 tablespoons butter ghee
1 onion, sliced
1 cup basmati rice
1 fresh bay leaf, bruised
1 cinnamon stick
4 whole cloves
12 cardamom pods, crushed
8 oz. peeled, seeded pumpkin
finely sliced zest and juice of 2 oranges

carrot and coconut kashumber

3 tablespoons unsweetened flaked coconut
1½ cups coarsely grated carrots,
½ cup roasted peanuts, chopped
freshly squeezed juice of 2 limes
½ teaspoon salt
2 chiles, seeded and chopped
2 tablespoons peanut oil
1 teaspoon cumin seeds
1 teaspoon black mustard seeds

onion and tomato kashumber

2 red onions, finely sliced
2 tomatoes, sliced
1 teaspoon toasted sesame seeds
1 tablespoon brown sugar

cucumber raita

1 small cucumber, cut into cubes
2 garlic cloves, crushed
1 tablespoon chopped fresh mint
½ cup thick plain yogurt
1 tablespoon peanut oil
1 tablespoon mustard seeds

serves 4

Kashumbers are fresh, spicy salads served as part of an Indian meal. A raita is also a salad, but is always dressed with yogurt—and makes a delicious, cooling cure for an overindulgence in chiles.

To make the pulao, heat the butter ghee in a pan, add the onion, and sauté until deep golden brown. Add the rice, bay leaf, cinnamon, cloves, and black seeds from the cardamom pods. Sauté for another 2 minutes.

Cut the pumpkin into ½-inch dice, and add to the pan with 2 cups boiling salted water. Return to a boil, cover, and reduce the heat to as low as possible. Cook, undisturbed, for 10 minutes. Add the orange zest and juice, cover, cook for 2–3 minutes more, turn off the heat, and set aside.

To make the carrot and coconut kashumber, put the coconut in a bowl, cover with boiling water, then drain. Put in a small bowl with the carrots, chopped peanuts, lime juice, salt, and chiles, and stir well.

Heat the peanut oil In a separate skillet. Add the cumin and mustard seeds, heat until they start to pop, then pour over the kashumber.

To make the onion and tomato kashumber, put the onions in a heatproof bowl and pour over boiling water. Refresh under cold water and pat dry with paper towels. Put in a small serving bowl, then add the tomatoes, sesame seeds, and brown sugar. Stir gently.

To make the raita, put the cucumber in a bowl and stir in the garlic, mint, and yogurt. Heat the peanut oil in a small skillet, add the mustard seeds, and sauté briefly until they pop. Spoon over the raita.

Serve the two kashumbers and the raita as accompaniments to the pulao.

african fish curry
with mustard seed rice

4 pieces of white fish, about 6 oz. each

1 tablespoon ground turmeric

1 teaspoon sea salt

3 tablespoons peanut oil

2 onions, sliced into rings

2 garlic cloves, crushed

2 tablespoons medium-hot curry paste

3 tablespoons sun-dried tomato paste

2 green jalapeño or serrano chiles

2 limes

1¾ cups canned coconut milk

mustard seed rice

2 tablespoons peanut oil

4 garlic cloves, crushed

1–2 tablespoons black mustard seeds

1 cinnamon stick, crushed (optional)

4 cups cooked white long grain rice

3–4 tablespoons seasoned fish stock

serves 4

Spice-trading nations like Portugal and India have had strong influences on the varied and lively cuisine of the east coast of Africa, producing interesting spice mixes. Use white fish such as snapper, bass, or haddock and a nonstick pan so the rice will reheat perfectly without sticking.

Pat the fish dry with paper towels, then rub it with the turmeric and salt. Heat the oil in a large skillet and brown the fish briefly on both sides. Remove the fish from the pan. Add the onions and garlic, sauté until browned, then sauté the curry paste and tomato paste for 1–2 minutes.

Halve the chiles lengthwise and seed them, then add them to the skillet together with the juice of 1 of the limes. Cook another 2 minutes, taking care not to burn. Add the coconut milk and heat to simmering. Add the fish and poach for 5–6 minutes on each side, adding a little water if the sauce becomes too thick.

To prepare the rice, heat the oil in a nonstick pan and sauté the garlic, mustard seeds, and cinnamon, if using, until the seeds start to pop and the garlic and cinnamon smell aromatic. Add the rice and stir-fry, moving it constantly, for 3–4 minutes. Add the seasoned stock, cover the pan, and heat the rice through.

Serve the seeded rice in deep bowls, with the curry spooned over and the remaining lime, cut into wedges or chunks.

Mee krob is the classic Thai fried noodle dish. It is very easy, but don't try to cook more than one skein of noodles at a time. Buy the noodles, rice vinegar, fish sauce, *tom yam* stock cubes, and tiny, fiercely hot, bird's eye chiles from an Asian market.

crispy thai noodles

8 oz. fine rice vermicelli noodles

peanut oil, for frying

3 eggs, beaten

½ cup sugar

⅓ cup rice vinegar

¼ cup light soy sauce

¼ cup Thai fish sauce

½ cup spicy stock, such as stock made from *tom yam stock* cubes

1 tablespoon mild paprika

2 teaspoons coriander seeds, crushed

8 oz. uncooked shrimp, shelled and deveined

4 skinless, boneless chicken breasts, finely sliced

1½ cups fresh bean sprouts

6 scallions, sliced lengthwise

3–4 bird's eye chiles, sliced crosswise

a bunch of cilantro, chopped

serves 4–6

Separate the layered skeins of noodles without breaking them. Cook one skein at a time. Pour about 2 inches peanut oil into a large wok and heat to 375°F, or until one strand puffs up immediately. Set a large metal strainer over a heatproof bowl. Put crumpled paper towels on a tray, ready for draining the fried noodles.

Using tongs, add a skein of noodles to the very hot oil. Cook for 10 seconds until puffed up and slightly browned, then turn it over carefully with tongs. Cook the second side, then set it on the paper towels. Repeat until all the noodles have been cooked. If there is any dark debris in the oil at any time, pour all the oil through the strainer into the heatproof bowl, discard the debris, and return the oil to the wok. Reheat the oil and continue cooking the remaining noodles. Pour out the hot oil, return the cooked noodles to the empty wok, and keep them warm.

Heat a small frying pan, add 1 tablespoon of hot oil, then half the eggs. Cook the omelet briefly on both sides. Remove and repeat with the remaining mixture. Roll up the omelets, slice into strips, and set aside.

Wipe out the pan and add the sugar, vinegar, soy and fish sauces, stock, paprika, and coriander seeds. Heat, stirring, until syrupy. Add the shrimp and poach until firm. Remove and set aside. Cook the chicken in the same way. Increase the heat, add the bean sprouts, scallions, omelet, and shrimp, and toss gently. Tip the mixture over the hot noodles in the large wok. Turn the noodles to coat, breaking them as little as possible. Add the chiles and cilantro leaves, and serve hot.

jambalaya
with andouille and shrimp

3 tablespoons canola or corn oil

2 tablespoons all-purpose flour (optional)

12 oz. pork shoulder, boneless pork chops, or tenderloin cut into 1-inch chunks

12 oz. spicy pork link sausage, such as andouille or chorizo, cut into 1-inch chunks

8 boneless, skinless chicken thighs

2 celery stalks, sliced

1 large onion, sliced

4 garlic cloves, crushed

1 green bell pepper, seeded, cored, and diced, or 2 seeded jalapeño chiles

1 bouquet garni (a bundle of fresh bay, thyme, parsley, and sage, tied together)

1 teaspoon hot red pepper flakes

1 lb. ripe fleshy red tomatoes, chopped

2½ cups white long-grain rice

4 cups boiling chicken or pork stock

4 oz. smoked ham, in long slices

8 oz. uncooked shrimp, shell-on

sea salt and freshly ground black pepper

serves 4–6

The word *jambalaya* is Louisiana Creole: *jam* is from *jambón*, the French word for "ham," *à la* means "of" or "with," and *ya* is an old African word for "rice." Jambalaya is related to pilafs, Caribbean pilaus and Spanish paella. It includes the Southern culinary "trinity" of celery, green bell peppers, and onion, and the brown roux of butter and flour, that pivotal element in Southern cooking.

Heat the oil in a large, heavy, flameproof casserole. Stir in the flour, if using, and cook to a golden-brown roux. Add the pork and sausage and cook, stirring and turning, for 6–7 minutes until brown. Remove with a slotted spoon and keep hot.

Add the chicken and sauté until golden brown and firm. Return the pork and sausage to the pan, add the celery, onion, garlic, green pepper or chiles, bouquet garni, and pepper flakes. Stir for 2 minutes more. Add the tomatoes and rice and stir until the rice is well coated. Add the hot stock, return to the boil, cover, and reduce to a gentle simmer. Cook undisturbed for 10 minutes, then add the ham and shrimp.

Cover and cook for another 4–5 minutes until the shrimp are pink and firm, the ham hot, the liquid almost completely absorbed, and the chunks of meat plump and tender. Stir gently. Cover the pan and let stand for 3 minutes with the heat turned off. Serve from the casserole.

seared swordfish
with wild rice and black bean salsa

4 swordfish steaks,
about 6 oz. each, cut about ½ inch thick

6 garlic cloves, cut into 5–6 slivers

sea salt and freshly ground black pepper

black bean salsa

¾ cup dried small black beans,
turtle beans, or kidney beans
(or 14 oz. canned black beans)

1 onion, quartered

1 bouquet garni or bunch of thyme

1 cup wild rice

½ cup chopped fresh cilantro

2 scallions, chopped

2 hot chiles, seeded and chopped

passionfruit and lime marinade

1 teaspoon sea salt

pulp, seeds, and juice of 6 passionfruit

1 teaspoon cumin seeds, crushed

2 red bell peppers, seeded and diced

⅔ cup extra virgin olive oil

1 teaspoon peppercorns, crushed

freshly squeezed juice of 6 limes

serves 4–6

Modern Florida cooking is very adventurous: passionfruit and lime are used to marinate the fish, and then added to the dressing. Wild rice is native to America, and makes a delicious, modern salsa when mixed with black beans and the spicy, fruity marinade.

To make the salsa, first soak the dried beans overnight in cold water to cover. Next day, drain the soaked beans and add boiling water to cover the beans by 3 inches. Add the onion and bouquet garni. Bring to a boil, then simmer partially covered for 1¼–1½ hours until the beans are soft enough to squash easily. After 45 minutes, put the wild rice in a saucepan with 4 cups boiling water. Return to a boil, cover, and simmer for 40–45 minutes until the grains are tender and some are splitting at the ends. Let stand for about 10 minutes, then drain.

Make 8 cuts in each fish steak, 4 on each side, and insert slivers of garlic.

To make the marinade, mix the salt, passionfruit, cumin, red bell pepper, oil, pepper, and half the lime juice. Beat briefly. When the rice is half cooked, pour the mixture over the fish and let marinate for 20 minutes.

Reserve ½ cup of the beans and put the remainder in a bowl with the rice.

Boil the marinade in a pan for 1 minute. Add the remaining lime juice. Pour half this mixture into a bowl, and stir the remainder through the rice and beans. To finish the salsa, add the cilantro, scallions, chiles, and reserved beans to the bowl of marinade. Season generously with salt and pepper.

Season the fish, then cook on a preheated grill or stove-top grill pan for 2½–3 minutes—no longer or it will dry out. Set the fish on the rice-bean base, add the salsa, and serve hot, warm, or cool, but not chilled.

A classic dish, usually made in three or four separate operations, is slightly simplified here into a one-pan dish. It is great party food that looks impressive, but is easy once the initial stages are complete.

chicken and orange pulau
with almonds and pistachios

2 unwaxed oranges, washed and dried

¾ cup sugar

2 large pinches saffron threads or 4 pinches saffron powder

4 tablespoons butter or butter ghee

1 cup blanched almonds

4–6 boneless, skinless breasts of chicken, each cut into 4 pieces

2 onions, sliced into rings

2¼ cups white basmati rice

¼ cup pistachio nuts, blanched and peeled

sea salt and freshly ground black pepper

6–8 sprigs of mint, to serve

serves 4–6

Using a zester or canelle knife, remove the orange zest in long shreds or, alternatively, use a vegetable peeler, then slice the strips into fine shreds. Blanch by pouring over boiling water, then refresh in cold water and drain.

Put the sugar in a saucepan with the orange zest and about ¾ cup orange juice and boil for 5–8 minutes, until thick and syrupy. Add the saffron, stir, and set aside.

Heat the butter in a large, flameproof casserole. Briefly cook the almonds until golden, remove with a slotted spoon, and set aside. Add the chicken, brown for about 2–3 minutes on each side, then remove and set aside.

Add the onions and cook over moderate heat until softened and translucent. Return the chicken to the pan, add salt, pepper, and 1 quart boiling water, then stir to dissolve the sediment. Stir in the rice and return to the boil. Cover with a lid, reduce to a simmer, then cook gently for 12–15 minutes on top of the stove or 35–45 minutes in a preheated oven at 300°F. Remove the lid: the rice should be fairly plump and tender and the liquid absorbed.

Sprinkle with the almonds, pistachios, and saffron syrup mixture, reserving the zest. Cover and cook again for 5 minutes on top of the stove or 10–15 minutes in the oven. Add the reserved zest and mint and serve hot from the casserole.

Peas or beans with rice is one of the world's greatest food combinations. Depending on the culture and location, you could use almost any kind of dried bean. See the note below for the different soaking and cooking times needed for each variety. In this recipe, the hot Caribbean chillies are left whole but pierced, to provide fruitiness as well as heat.

2½ cups dried peas or beans*

2 habanero or Scotch bonnet chiles, pierced several times with a needle

1 onion, quartered

1½ lb. smoked shoulder bacon or ham, or 1 bacon or ham hock

2½ cups white long-grain rice, or white easy-cook rice

1¾ cups canned coconut milk

chile sauce

4 garlic cloves

2 medium hot green chiles, such as serrano or jalapeño

a bunch of fresh oregano

a bunch of fresh flat-leaf parsley

8 scallions, chopped

freshly squeezed juice of 5 limes or 3 lemons

1 tablespoon mixed French mustard

salt, to taste

serves 6–8

Dried peas or beans should be soaked overnight, then cooked, according to their variety, as described right.

rice and peas
with hot jamaican chile sauce

To soak the peas or beans, cover with cold water and leave overnight, or pour over boiling water, cover with a lid, and soak for 1 hour. Drain. If using red beans, boil vigorously for 15 minutes, then discard the water before final cooking.

Put the soaked beans in a large saucepan with boiling water to cover by 3 inches. Add the chiles, onion, and bacon. Boil for 10 minutes, partially cover with a lid, and cook at a moderate boil according to the times in the note below, or until fairly tender.

Add the rice and coconut milk. Simmer, partially covered with a lid, for about 17 minutes. Drain off any liquid into a pan, reduce to 2 tablespoons, and return to the beans. Remove and discard the chiles. Remove the meat, slice it, then return it to the pan.

To make the chile sauce, put the garlic, green chiles, oregano, parsley, scallions, lime or lemon juice, mustard, and salt in a food processor. Blend briefly.

Serve the rice and peas in bowls with chile sauce on top, and serve the remaining sauce separately.

Note Cooking times for presoaked peas or beans are 40–50 minutes for red or black kidney beans, 1¼–1½ hours for black-eyed and gungo peas, 1½–2 hours for black turtle beans. Red kidney beans must be boiled hard for 15 minutes first and the water discarded.

8 small squid

2 lb. live mussels, scrubbed

⅔ cup white wine

1½ quarts well-seasoned fish stock

6 tablespoons extra virgin olive oil

24 uncooked medium shrimp, shell-on

1 lb. chicken, cut into chunks

1½ lb. chorizo or other spicy pork sausage, such as kielbasa or andouille, cut into chunks

1 large Spanish onion, sliced

2 red bell peppers, seeded and sliced

1 whole garlic head, trimmed

2 large fleshy tomatoes, chopped

2 teaspoons sweet paprika

2½ cups paella rice or risotto rice

1½ cups shelled fava beans or peas

a pinch of saffron threads

½ cup fresh flat-leaf parsley, snipped with kitchen shears, to serve (optional)

serves 8

Spain's paella is a handsome, one-pan dish. Use a round, short-grain paella rice such as calasparra, or an Italian risotto-style rice. Allow two handfuls, or 3–4 oz. per person for paella rice, and cook for about 18 minutes (or 25–30 for calasparra, which may also need more water). The fiercer heat, the lack of stirring and the fact that the rice goes directly into the boiling liquid all make this very different from a risotto.

spanish paella

To prepare the squid, gently pull the head and body apart. Cut off and reserve the tentacles from the head section. Remove and discard the plastic-like 'quill' and soft roe from the body. Remove the skin if preferred.

Discard any open or heavy mussels. Put the remaining mussels in a saucepan with the white wine. Boil fiercely, covered, until they open (about 1–2 minutes). Discard any that don't open. Remove them one by one and set aside. Strain the liquid into the stock.

Heat half the oil in a large paella pan or skillet. Add the shrimp and squid and fry briefly until barely set. Remove and set aside. Add the chicken and chorizo, and brown over moderate heat for 10–12 minutes.

Add the onion, bell peppers, garlic, tomatoes, stock, and half the paprika. Bring to a rapid boil, stir in the rice, reduce the heat to a gentle simmer, and cook, uncovered, without stirring, for 16–18 minutes or until the rice is cooked.

Add the fava beans, saffron, and the remaining paprika and oil. Stir, add all the seafood, then cook for 8–10 minutes on very low heat until the rice is fully cooked and dry. Add extra stock or water as necessary. Serve, sprinkled with parsley.

sides

moroccan couscous
with rice, lemon, and tahini

1 cucumber

8–12 baby zucchini, sliced

4 carrots, sliced diagonally

1¼ cups white long-grain rice

3¾ cups hot, seasoned vegetable stock

⅓ cup instant couscous

chermoula marinade

2 garlic cloves, chopped

2 teaspoons harissa paste

1 teaspoon powdered cumin

1 teaspoon mild paprika

a bunch of cilantro, snipped

⅓ cup extra virgin olive oil

tahini sauce

2 garlic cloves, crushed

1 teaspoon ground cumin

½ cup tahini (roasted sesame) paste

freshly squeezed juice of 2 lemons

to serve

a large bunch of fresh mint

10–12 small black olives

½ preserved lemon, chopped,
or lemon zest

serves 4

A simplified version of the classic Moroccan dish *Couscous aux Sept Légumes*. Pickled lemons, instant couscous, and harissa, the fiery red North African spice paste, can be found in North African, Middle Eastern, and French food stores and larger supermarkets.

Peel and seed the cucumber and cut into chunks. Mix the chermoula ingredients in a bowl, add the cucumber, zucchini and carrots, and toss until well coated. Let stand.

Put the rice and stock in a medium saucepan, return to a boil, cover with a lid, reduce to simmering, and cook, undisturbed, for 6 minutes. Stir in the couscous and arrange the chermoula-coated vegetables evenly on top. Sprinkle with the remaining chermoula and other juices. Cover and cook, undisturbed, for 8–10 minutes or until the vegetables are succulent, the couscous and rice are tender, and all the liquid has been absorbed.

Reserve 3–4 sprigs of the mint and chop the rest. Put the vegetables on one side of the serving dish. Stir the olives, lemon pieces (or zest), and mint through the rice mixture. Spoon onto the serving dish beside the vegetables, and let cool slightly.

To make the tahini sauce, put the garlic, cumin, tahini, and lemon juice in a blender and purée to a thick cream. Trickle in 8–10 tablespoons ice water, a spoonful at a time, to form a pale creamy dressing.

To serve, trickle the sauce over the whole dish (warm or cool, but not chilled), add the reserved mint sprigs, and serve the remaining dressing separately.

spicy seeded pilaf
with okra and spinach

The cuisine of the state of Gujerat, in northwest India, contains interesting spice combinations, a legacy of its position on a major ancient caravan route taking spices and other goods from the East to the West. Gujerat is largely vegetarian, and rice dishes are much loved.

1 onion

8 oz. pattypan squash

1–1½ teaspoons hot chile powder

½ teaspoon ground turmeric

2 tablespoons peanut oil

1 teaspoon poppy seeds, crushed

1 teaspoon cumin seeds, crushed

1 teaspoon coriander seeds, crushed

½ teaspoon asafoetida (optional)

4 garlic cloves, crushed

¼ teaspoon salt

1¼ cups white basmati rice

2½ cups boiling vegetable stock

2 dried bay leaves (optional)

2 tablespoons coconut cream

4 oz. okra, trimmed

4 oz. baby spinach

½ cup green peas (optional)

2 oz. frozen flaked coconut

serves 4

Slice the onion lengthwise into thin segments. Toss the onion and squash in the chile powder and turmeric. Heat the oil in a skillet and sauté the vegetables for 1–2 minutes or until aromatic. Add the poppy, cumin and coriander seeds, the asafoetida, if using, the garlic, and salt. Cook over moderate heat until the seeds begin to crackle and pop and become aromatic.

Stir in the rice. Sauté for another minute, stirring gently, then add the stock, bay leaves, if using, and the coconut. Cover and reduce the heat to simmering, then cook undisturbed for 8 minutes.

Add the okra, spinach, green peas, and coconut shreds. Cover and cook for a further 4–5 minutes until the rice is tender but dry. Remove the bay leaves, stir well, and serve the rice with other vegetarian dishes, or with meat, poultry, or fish curries and accompaniments such as the kashumbers and raita on page 30.

pearl divers' rice
with saffron and honey

The author and Middle Eastern food expert, Tess Mallos, described this ancient rice dish as one which perfectly satisfied the calorie and blood-sugar needs of Bahrain's pearl divers. They dived, in hazardous conditions, to considerable depths for 10 minutes at a time. The combination of rich, sweet, and savory flavors is remarkable. Traditionally this dish would be served with lamb or seafood dishes.

a pinch of saffron threads

8 green cardamom pods, crushed

2 tablespoons rose water

1 quart boiling lamb or chicken stock

2¼ cups white basmati rice

2 onions, sliced into rings

2 teaspoons salt

3 oz. clear honey

4 tablespoons butter, chopped into 8 pieces

a large bunch of fresh parsley, dill, or mint, snipped with kitchen shears (optional)

serves 4–6

Put the saffron in a small, heatproof bowl, then add the black seeds from the cardamom pods, the rose water and ¼ cup of the boiling stock. Set over a saucepan of boiling water while you cook the rice.

Put the rice, onions, and salt in a large saucepan, and pour in the remaining boiling stock. Return to a boil, cover, reduce to a gentle simmer, and cook for 10 minutes or until almost all the liquid has been absorbed.

Pour the saffron mixture on top and trickle the honey over the surface. Push 8 holes in the rice down to the base of the pan and add a bit of butter to each. Cover the pan again and simmer for a further 5 minutes. Remove from the heat, wrap the pan in a cloth, let stand for another 10 minutes, then serve hot, sprinkled with parsley, dill, or mint, if using.

This casual, homey dish is easy to make as long as the rice has been recently cooked and cool (neither chilled nor still hot) and you keep the eggs creamy. My version stirs sauces through the rice, rather than serving separately—regarded as sacrilege by purists, but it is commonplace, even so.

classic cantonese fried rice
with scallions, ham, and crab

4 oz. cooked smoked ham

4 oz. cooked crabmeat

4 oz. canned water chestnuts

8 scallions

¼ cup peanut oil

2 onions, chopped

8 cups cooked, cool, long-grain white rice (from 2½ cups raw rice)

3 eggs, beaten

1 tablespoon tomato paste or tomato juice

2 tablespoons black bean sauce

2 tablespoons light soy sauce

1 tablespoon sweet chile sauce

a large bunch of flat-leaf parsley, snipped with kitchen shears

sea salt and freshly ground black pepper

serves 4–5

Finely slice the ham and shred the crabmeat. Drain and slice the water chestnuts and finely slice the scallions diagonally, then set aside until you are ready to assemble the dish.

Heat a wok or deep skillet. Add the oil and, when hot, add the onions and stir-fry over medium heat until softened and translucent. Add the crabmeat and ham and cook for a further 2 minutes, uncovered, until hot.

Add the cooked rice, heat, and stir, then cover and cook, undisturbed, for about 5 minutes or until heated through. Add the water chestnuts.

Season the eggs with salt and pepper and pour them into a hollow in the center of the rice. Stir around the edges, until just beginning to set, then stir the egg from the middle to the outer edge so the egg sets quickly, but is still moist.

Add the tomato paste, black bean, soy, and chile sauces to the rice, then add the scallions, tossing quickly into the hot rice.

To serve, sprinkle the parsley over the dish. Serve hot while the egg is still creamy: the mixture will continue cooking on the plate. Serve with other Asian dishes.

indonesian fried rice

4 cups cooked white long-grain rice

about ½ cup peanut oil

12 oz. steak from pork or beef rump

¼ cup ready-fried onion flakes (or kalonji)

3 eggs

1 teaspoon hot red pepper flakes

½ teaspoon salt

2 onions, chopped

3–4 garlic cloves, crushed or finely sliced

2 tablespoons Asian fish sauce*

8 oz. uncooked shrimp tails, shelled and deveined

4 inches cucumber, cut into matchsticks

1 carrot, finely sliced and blanched

1 cup fresh or frozen peas or beans, blanched

2 tablespoons light soy sauce

4 scallions, finely sliced lengthwise

serves 4

*If you can find authentic Indonesian shrimp paste (blachan), use that instead. It has an intense flavor, so 1 teaspoon is sufficient. It is available in some Southeast Asian or Chinese markets.

Like Cantonese fried rice, the Indonesian equivalent *nasi goreng* has traveled all over the world and been adapted along the way. Some Indonesians maintain that it originated in China, but it has always been associated with the *rijsttafel* (rice table) of Dutch colonial rule. It can combine cooked rice, omelet strips (in this case chile-seasoned as well), vegetables, meat, fish, and aromatics.

Cook the rice 2–3 hours ahead. When ready to prepare the fried rice, heat 1 tablespoon of the oil in a wok or skillet and cook the steak over high heat to seal on both sides—do not cook it fully. Let cool, cut into thin strips, and set aside.

If using dried onion flakes (not the ready-cooked ones), sauté them in 1 tablespoon of the oil until crisp and brown. Set aside. Put the eggs, pepper flakes, and salt in a bowl and beat with a fork.

Add a further 1 tablespoon oil to the pan, pour in half the egg mixture, adding a little more oil if needed, and make a thin omelet. Turn it over and cook until pale gold on both sides. Make a second omelet with the remaining mixture. Roll up both omelets, slice finely, and set aside.

Put the chopped onions, garlic, and shrimp paste in a food processor and purée to a coarse paste. Heat 2 tablespoons of the remaining oil in a large wok or deep skillet, add the garlic mixture, and stir-fry for 3–4 minutes until cooked and dryish.

Add the remaining 2 tablespoons of oil, the meat, shrimp, cucumber, carrot, and peas or beans. Stir-fry for 2 minutes, then add the rice. Mix well, then sprinkle with soy sauce. Cover and cook briefly to reheat all ingredients, sprinkling in a little water as needed to help to create the necessary steam. Top with the scallions and onion flakes and serve with other Asian dishes.

sweet things

Traditionally this dish used almond "milk" obtained from grinding blanched almonds, infusing them in liquid, then squeezing out the juice to use in the dish. The almonds were then discarded. Almonds are expensive, so I infuse them, but do not discard them. This gives a slightly grittier, grainier version, but delicious nonetheless. Some people loathe the marzipan taste of almond extract, so you could use Noyau or Amaretto liqueur instead.

almond rice custard
with berries or pomegranate seeds

¼ cup white long-grain rice

3 cups milk

1 cup very fresh flaked almonds, ground to a powder in a blender

a large pinch of salt

⅔ cup light cream

⅓ cup sugar

¼ teaspoon pure almond extract or 2–3 teaspoons Noyau liqueur

to serve

6 oz. fresh berries, such as blackberries or raspberries, or 1 ripe pomegranate

2 tablespoons toasted almond flakes (optional)

2 tablespoons confectioners' sugar (optional)

serves 4–6

Put the rice in a clean coffee grinder and grind to a powder.

Put 1 cup of the milk in a saucepan and boil until frothing. Put the ground almonds in a bowl and pour the boiling milk over the top. Stir well, then pour the mixture into a blender or food processor. Blend for 10 seconds.

Put the salt, ground rice, and cream in a bowl and stir well. Heat the remaining milk until frothing, then pour it over the ground rice mixture, then beat well. Return to the pan, bring to a boil, then simmer, stirring, for 2–3 minutes or until thickened. Add the unstrained almond-milk mixture, and the sugar.

Continue cooking and stirring briefly, then remove from the heat. Cool the custard over ice water. When almost cold, stir in almond extract to taste. Pour into 4–6 small dishes, bowls, or glasses. Chill.

If using berries, remove the stems and pile on top of the custard. If using a pomegranate, break it open, remove the clumps of seeds, and pile as before.

Sprinkle with nuts and dust with confectioners' sugar, if using.

black coconut rice
with red berries or tropical fruits

2 cups Thai or Indonesian glutinous "black" rice (actually deep red)

2 slit vanilla beans

1¼ cups dark brown sugar

1¾ cups canned coconut milk

to serve

a selection of fresh red berries

confectioners' sugar, for dusting (optional)

serves 4

Black rice, grown in Southeast Asia, is actually a dark, garnet red. Red berries are easy to find, but you might like to use a mixture of chopped tropical fruit instead.

Put the rice and vanilla beans in a saucepan with 1 quart boiling water and return to a boil. Cover, reduce the heat to low, and cook, undisturbed, for about 25 minutes, or until almost dry.

Remove the pan from the heat and let stand for 10 minutes. Remove the vanilla beans. Add the sugar and ½ cup of the coconut milk. Stir until dissolved.

Serve the rice on small plates, top with berries, and pour over some of the coconut milk—serve the rest in a small pitcher. Pile the fruit on top of the rice and dust with confectioners' sugar, if using.

1¾ cups shredded coconut

2 eggs, separated

1¼ cups sugar,
plus 1 tablespoon extra

½ cup self-rising flour

1 cup plus 2 tablespoons
rice flour

1 teaspoon baking powder

1 teaspoon cardamom seeds
(from 8–10 green cardamom pods,
lightly crushed)

½ teaspoon ground cloves

½ teaspoon ground cinnamon

½ teaspoon grated nutmeg

1 teaspoon double-strength
orange flower water

½ cup cup cashews, chopped

finely sliced zest and juice of
1 unwaxed orange (keep separate)

*a loaf pan, 16 x 5 inches, greased
with butter and lined with paper*

makes 2 lb. loaf

This densely textured loaf, based on a Sri Lankan recipe, uses a mixture of wheat and rice flour to achieve its excellent taste and texture. You can vary the spices, and chopped almonds or walnuts could replace the cashews. Lemon zest and juice could also be substituted for orange. Serve in generous slices spread with mascarpone, cream cheese, or butter. It can also double as a quick dessert, served with snowy coconut sorbet in generous scoops.

spicy coconut loaf
with cashews and cardamom

Put the coconut and 1½ cups water in a blender (in 2 batches, if necessary) and blend until creamy. Set aside.

Using an electric mixer, beat the egg yolks, 1 tablespoon of the coconut mixture, and the 1¼ cups sugar until light and fluffy. Add the remaining coconut mixture and beat well by hand. Sift in the flour, rice flour, and baking powder, then add the black cardamom seeds, cloves, cinnamon, nutmeg, orange flower water, cashews, and orange zest—but not the juice—and stir well.

Put the egg whites in a clean bowl and beat until stiff peaks form. Add the extra sugar and beat again until the meringue is stiff and shiny. Fold it gently into the coconut mixture. Pour into the prepared loaf pan. Bake toward the top of a preheated oven at 325°F for 1 hour 10 minutes, or until risen and golden brown on top. A skewer inserted in the center of the loaf should come out clean.

Pour the juice over the top. Let stand 15 minutes, then invert onto a wire rack. Cool a little and serve warm, or cool completely and store in an airtight container.

Rice flour, available at natural food stores, is used here with an equal quantity of all-purpose flour, giving a delicate crispness to these little cookies. They are delicious with coffee or mint tea, or served with ice creams, puddings, or sorbets. Edible rice paper is often used in cooking or wrapping cookies or candies.

spiced shortbread cookies
with rose water and pistachios

2 sticks plus 2 tablespoons salted butter, at room temperature

1 teaspoon cardamom seeds (from 8–10 green cardamom pods, lightly crushed)

⅔ cup sugar

1 cup plus 1 tablespoon rice flour

1 cup all-purpose flour, plus extra for mixing

¼ cup blanched, peeled pistachios, finely slivered or chopped, plus 2 teaspoons slivered, to decorate

¼ teaspoon salt

¼ teaspoon baking powder

1 teaspoon double-strength rose water or pure almond extract

parchment paper or rice paper

a baking tray

makes 32

Cut the butter into small pieces and put in a food processor with the cardamom seeds. Pulse in small bursts, gradually adding the sugar through the feed tube until the mixture becomes light and fluffy.

Put the rice flour, all-purpose flour, pistachios, salt, and baking powder in a bowl and stir well. Add a quarter of this mixture at a time down the feed tube, using the pulse button, to form a soft, crumbly dough. Alternatively, use a bowl and whisk.

Transfer the dough to a floured work surface and mix in the rose water by hand. Put the dough on a sheet of parchment paper or rice paper, and pat out into a rectangle about 10 x 8 inches. Using a knife, mark into 32 even rectangles, about 2 x 1 inch each. Prick all over with a fork. Transfer to a baking tray. Sprinkle a few slivers of pistachio over each cookie, then bake in a preheated oven at 250°F for 1 hour or until pale gold, crisp, but not deep brown.

Remove from the oven and separate each cookie, cutting cleanly through the rice paper as well, if using. Let cool on a wire rack and, when completely cold, store in an airtight container.

index

conversion charts

Weights and measures have been rounded up or
down slightly to make measuring easier.

Volume equivalents:

American	Metric	Imperial
1 teaspoon	5 ml	
1 tablespoon	15 ml	
¼ cup	60 ml	2 fl.oz.
⅓ cup	75 ml	2½ fl.oz.
½ cup	125 ml	4 fl.oz.
⅔ cup	150 ml	5 fl.oz. (¼ pint)
¾ cup	175 ml	6 fl.oz.
1 cup	250 ml	8 fl.oz.

Weight equivalents:

Imperial	Metric
1 oz.	25 g
2 oz.	50 g
3 oz.	75 g
4 oz.	125 g
5 oz.	150 g
6 oz.	175 g
7 oz.	200 g
8 oz. (½ lb.)	250 g
9 oz.	275 g
10 oz.	300 g
11 oz.	325 g
12 oz.	375 g
13 oz.	400 g
14 oz.	425 g
15 oz.	475 g
16 oz. (1 lb.)	500 g
2 1b.	1 kg

Measurements:

Inches	Cm
¼ inch	5 mm
½ inch	1 cm
¾ inch	1.5 cm
1 inch	2.5 cm
2 inches	5 cm
3 inches	7 cm
4 inches	10 cm
5 inches	12 cm
6 inches	15 cm
7 inches	18 cm
8 inches	20 cm
9 inches	23 cm
10 inches	25 cm
11 inches	28 cm
12 inches	30 cm

Oven temperatures:

110°C	(225°F)	Gas ¼
120°C	(250°F)	Gas ½
140°C	(275°F)	Gas 1
150°C	(300°F)	Gas 2
160°C	(325°F)	Gas 3
180°C	(350°F)	Gas 4
190°C	(375°F)	Gas 5
200°C	(400°F)	Gas 6
220°C	(425°F)	Gas 7
230°C	(450°F)	Gas 8
240°C	(475°F)	Gas 9